TAROT CARDS

The Advanced Guide for Learning the Secrets of Tarot Cards

(Learn the Tarot for Beginners & Advanced)

Lisa Navarra

Published by Sharon Lohan

© **Lisa Navarra**

All Rights Reserved

Tarot Cards: The Advanced Guide for Learning the Secrets of Tarot Cards (Learn the Tarot for Beginners & Advanced)

ISBN 978-1-990334-63-4

All rights reserved. No part of this guide may be reproduced in any form without permission in writing from the publisher except in the case of brief quotations embodied in critical articles or reviews.

Legal & Disclaimer

The information contained in this book is not designed to replace or take the place of any form of medicine or professional medical advice. The information in this book has been provided for educational and entertainment purposes only.

The information contained in this book has been compiled from sources deemed reliable, and it is accurate to the best of the Author's knowledge; however, the Author cannot guarantee its accuracy and validity and cannot be held liable for any errors or omissions. Changes are periodically made to this book. You must consult your doctor or get professional medical advice before using any of the suggested remedies, techniques, or information in this book.

Upon using the information contained in this book, you agree to hold harmless the Author from and against any damages, costs, and expenses, including any legal fees potentially resulting from the application of any of the information provided by this guide. This disclaimer applies to any damages or injury caused by the use and application, whether directly or indirectly, of any advice or information presented, whether for breach of contract, tort, negligence, personal injury, criminal intent, or under any other cause of action.

You agree to accept all risks of using the information presented inside this book. You need to consult a professional medical practitioner in order to ensure you are both able and healthy enough to participate in this program.

Table of Contents

INTRODUCTION 1

CHAPTER 1: THE MYTH BUSTERS: THE TRUTH BEHIND THE MOST POPULAR MYTHS 4

CHAPTER 2: INTRODUCING THE MYSTERIOUS TAROT 17

CHAPTER 3: AN INTRODUCTION TO TAROT 23

CHAPTER 4: A BASIC HISTORY.. 32

CHAPTER 5: TAROT AND ITS HISTORY................................ 40

CHAPTER 6: WHAT IS TAROT? 77

CHAPTER 7: SUIT OF CUPS 86

CHAPTER 8: HISTORY OF TAROT CARDS............................ 92

CHAPTER 9: UNDERSTANDING TAROT............................... 96

CHAPTER 10: TYPES OF READINGS................................. 109

CHAPTER 11: CUPS AND WANDS 117

CHAPTER 12: THE CONNECTION BETWEEN TAROT AND ASTROLOGY CARD COMBINATION 123

CHAPTER 13: THE KEY TO THE MAJOR ARCANA............. 128

CHAPTER 14: TAROT, NUMEROLOGY, AND QABALAH ... 137

CONCLUSION... 159

Introduction

People always look at seeking knowledge about what they do not know and expanding their horizons. But most of all, they are curious to know what makes a person tick. They would like to understand the dangers or the happiness that they or any other person might face in the future or the present. We are eager to know our futures and are always looking at finding a link between our past and present. We believe that this helps us understand our future – learn about our personal and professional lives and also any obstacles we might face. The easiest way to do this is through Tarot reading. This is an age-old art that helps us depict the future and well-being of a person. Can you believe that it was in fact a card game?

This book is the ultimate guide to you if you are a beginner. It could also be sued to refresh your memory if you are looking at a Tarot reading. It provides you with all the information that you need to have if you are looking at giving any person a Tarot reading. Once you finish the book, you will be able to understand and learn more about yourself and others through Tarot card reading.

The various chapters tell you about the different cards that are available and the cards that you will need to use depending on the situation. There is a set of instructions that you must keep in mind at all times when using the Tarot cards. The book provides you with the information on how you can use these Tarot cards as well. The different chapters tell you how the different tarot cards can be interpreted and what they mean. There is also a sample reading provided to help you understand how a reading is usually done.

Good luck to you in your fortune telling adventures!

Chapter 1: The Myth Busters: The Truth Behind The Most Popular Myths

Since this book is intended to be a beginner's guide in the art of tarot reading, it is important to set things straight from the very start. I am sure you have heard or read things like "One doesn't need to know (as in learn) anything about tarot in order to practice it. It just comes naturally for those who really have this gift." What a mysterious (or even magical, if you prefer) world these people are describing. Unfortunately (or not), the truth is far from that. As much as we would like to believe in such ideas, they are only part of good advertising that has the power to draw people's attention.

Years of experience have shown that there is no such thing as a good tarot reader who does not have the minimum information about the origins, the history, and the real meanings of what this practice is about. For this reason, I must do my task correctly, and include this type of information as well. Because I promised in the introduction not to bore you with too many theoretical facts, I will use a diverting method – that of making you understand what tarot reading entails by learning about what it is not. Thus, I will further develop the list of myths that were only briefly mentioned in the previous section.

Myth #1 – There is no escape from what the cards will show you

I chose to put this one first because I think that this one thing must be known by everyone, before practicing or going for the first time to a tarot reader: no matter what question you have in your mind, or what sign appears on your cards, it's not an absolute fact that something is going to happen. In fact, the whole purpose of tarot reading is to have a deeper understanding of the situation of interest for you. Once you get the answer, you already start to change your perspective, one way or another, and the universe will work on the issue accordingly. In the same way, if, for example, you find out that a person has certain negative thoughts about you, it's not necessary for that person to always maintain this attitude or to put those thoughts into practice. Remember that we all have free will, and everything else is just to give us a little help.

Myth #2 – Tarot reading is the devil's tool; it can be labeled as "witchcraft"

I think we have all heard this at least one time in our lives. However, no matter how the myth is stated, tarot reading it is not evil. This is, of course, unless the reader is purposely up to some mischief, and misleads or lies to the seeker with the sole purpose of getting more money from him/her. Other than that, I imagine anything else. In the end, what you are trying to do is to find some answers to your questions; it's not like you have the power to do harm to another person through the cards.

So why do some people consider tarot to be witchcraft? The reason for this popular myth probably lies in the fact that the Catholic Church has banned tarot cards and tarot reading, and people have associated this act with some black power that supposedly belongs to the cards. But the church also banned gambling and standard playing cards. Are they evil too? Of course they are if their purpose is not directed towards anything good. And this is valid for absolutely all the objects in this world.

Myth #3 – You must perform occult rituals in order to get the best results

Just like the previous one, this myth has its origins in the same beliefs that tarot has something to do with black magic since it was banned by the church. But this is nothing more than pure nonsense. When performing the reading, the reader does not count on anything but his or her own knowledge and power to understand and connect the results. However, it is true that everyone can have their little rituals or order of doing things. But this is only because this is how they got accustomed over time and it helps them relax, be more confident, and help the person in front of them as much as they can.

Myth #4 – You will be a psychic or have psychic powers if you begin to practice with tarot cards (or, even better, a witch)

Wouldn't this be nice if it were true? This would mean that the reader's power does not end with the tarot cards and they can do or find out many more precise facts about the world. Unfortunately, this is not true. Learning to read these cards does not give you any kind of magical powers nor do they help you communicate with other dimensions. I don't deny that there are readers who have these powers, but they certainly did not start with this practice. Sorry if I just ruined your expectations for this book.

Myth #5 – You cannot use other tarot cards than the ones that have been given to you by another tarot reader

This idea is also related to the previous myths, implying that the cards have a certain magical power, which was generated by one factor in time and kept by generations and generations of "gifted tarot readers". If you are lucky enough to have a tarot reader in your family, I am sure that he or she has already explained to you that the things that matter are in your head, and not in a specific set of fabricated paper. There is nothing more than a strict emotional connection that can be created in this way. The myth that you should only practice tarot reading on old and specially-inherited tarot cards is, again, incredibly foolish.

Myth #6 – The power of the cards depends on how well you can take care of them and the powers they get in contact with

Well, this is true. You must take good care of them (and everything you own) in order to keep them away from getting ripped, dirty, misplaced, or who-knows-what-else. So it's nonetheless important to have an established place in the house where you keep them and a secure wrapping to protect them. Keeping them wrapped in black silk and a locked wooden box is also a myth that probably lasts from those times when you needed to hide the fact that you own these cards. Also, their power can't be affected by the seeker or any other person that touches them. Of course, there are people who can influence the act of reading, but this won't damage your cards in any way. However, if you prefer, there are certain cleansing methods that can help you remove any negative energy that might be attached to them.

Myth #7 – The cards can never make a mistake

If this was true, the world would probably be in a much better condition now. But this is not true. We would be naive to think that the answer obtained from a session of tarot reading is always the best one. As in any other area of life, errors can occur: because the reader did not concentrate, or did not use all the necessary information for that specific context, because the seeker did not put the question correctly, or a combination of all these reasons. The fact is that you should never perceive a result as something that is doomed to happen.

Myth #8 – If you get the Death card, that's it: pack up your things and get ready for the next life

If you are familiar with this idea, you are probably also familiar with those poor-quality movies or soap operas in which a troubled young woman would always want to find out about the person that was predestined for her. So, after the middle of the night, she would always go in a bad-famed area of the town, through dark and empty alleys to the house of an old, scary tarot reader. And, instead of discovering who loves her, the death card would always appear, the creepy music would intensify, and the woman would start crying because her end is close. We all know these scenes. But the truth is that the death card is no more than a sign that a change — of any nature — is about to happen in your life, and, moreover, that you are ready for this change. In other words, it might be interpreted as the "death" of one chapter or aspect from your life.

Myth #9 — You must never read the cards to yourself

Another myth that I've noticed is extremely popular is that if you are reading the cards for yourself, you are instantly bringing bad luck in your life. To this, I can only laugh, because, trust me, there is absolutely no difference in the outcome of a session with another person or just by yourself. However, I agree to some extent with this statement: sometimes, it can be difficult to be completely objective when you read for yourself, and you might be tempted to "see" the answer that you want to see. Other than this, there is no reason not to read to yourself.

Myth #10 – If the seeker or the reader does a single gesture wrong, the whole session is compromised

If the reader doesn't take the cards with the left hand first, if the seeker doesn't cut the cards with the right hand, if the reader does not look the seeker directly in the eyes, if they don't do this, if they don't do that, and so on. You can see my point here. All these are small superstitions that have probably formed by some person's habit or favorite way to do things. But there is no proven meaning for these gestures. Thus, if they are not part of the session, their absence could not interfere or produce any harm.

Myth #11 – Their origin can be traced back to ancient Egypt/ they are as old as the pyramids/ they were invented in the early Gypsy tradition

These and many other "origin myths" that circulate today are just that: myths with an unknown basis. Their purpose is to give this practice an even gloomier interpretation, but the factual history tells us clearly that they are not true. These cards were first invented in the 15th-century Italy, and, by then, they were nothing more than a regular card game. It is known that they were first created by an Italian artist who traced the images of the Visconti and Sforza families on a deck of cards. About a century later, the cards became tools of divination when different meanings began to be associated with each of the cards.

Chapter 2: Introducing The Mysterious Tarot

When one considers the tarot, they may have certain images in their mind. Perhaps the most likely image is one of an old gypsy woman, with a scarf on her head, laying down cards to reveal the secrets of the future.

The tarot is an ancient art that is now used for the purpose of fortune telling. Its origins are blurry and debateable, though most agree that they date back to the 15th Century. At that time, it is believed that the wealthy in Italy would come together and commission the creation of the stunning tarot decks. They would then play with these cards as you would with any interactive card game.

The tarot has connections that are rooted to the occult, as well as symbolism that helps to reveal what the future holds. It brings to light what would otherwise be mysterious. This connection to the occult was found in the late eighteenth and the nineteenth centuries. When the cards were examined, they appeared to tell a story that no one had considered. This meant that at this time, the tarot deck was acknowledged to be more than a basic card game.

Understanding Tarot Cards and Tarot Readings

Tarot reading is done using tarot cards, which are a special pack of cards that contain images and words on them. The key to unlocking the mystery of the tarot lies in being able to interpret the cards, so that they can reveal something about the future. When the tarot cards are being read, there are two people who are involved. The first person is known as the seeker, and they are the person who has a personal question for which they are hoping to get some answers. The other person is referred to as a reader, and they are the ones who will lay the cards on a surface in a certain formation which is referred to as a spread. From the spread, it will become easier to interpret the meanings behind the reading.

This can be done in several ways, though what the card reader needs is an active imagination, as well as the ability to think creatively. Then, it is imperative to understand what each of the symbols on the cards mean, and tap into intuition whenever an interpretation is necessary.

Over the years, most people have associated tarot cards with the dark side of the occult, attributing them to something that is evil and unsavoury. Despite this association, the use and interpretation of tarot cards continues to increase in popularity, and there is a fundamental reason for this occurrence.

Tarot cards are meant to reveal a message that is already there. They do not create a message or bring one up out of nothing. Rather, they clearly show what may be residing deep within ones subconscious, where our memories create associations which we are not sensitive enough to pick up and interpret. In daily life, it may be possible to switch off or run away from the conscious mind, but the unconscious mind remains ever present, and the tarot offers a clear avenue to unlock and discern its mysterious secrets.

Tarot Cards and the Subconscious Mind

For centuries, people have tried to tap into their subconscious mind, and the tarot card is one simple tool that can be used for this purpose. The tarot cards do not give every person who reads them the same message, and if you understand that these cards are tapping into your own subconscious and imagination, it will become clear why these cards tell individual seekers different stories.

What makes these cards applicable to so many different people is the connection that they create between human needs that are common in nature. These cards are reflective of both the emotions of a human being, as well as their thoughts.

Consider the law of attraction which has a premise that we attract things into our lives, including events and experiences. The same principle applies when dealing with tarot cards. When selecting cards for a reading, the reader will 'randomly' choose certain cards from the deck. Although the selection does seem random, it really is not as something that cannot be explained will lead a person to choose a particular card.

To get the most out of the cards, you need to open up your perception, particularly when it comes to looking deeper into the images that have been represented on the cards. The message that you receive is not a definite future that must happen, though it does give an idea of what could happen should most circumstances remain the same.

A typical sceptic will discount everything that the tarot deck attempts to communicate, yet, a seeker who trusts in what the cards have to reveal will find that their message is very close to the truth.

Over the years, the standard tarot deck has been recreated, so that today there are several types of tarot cards that one could choose from.

Chapter 3: An Introduction To Tarot

Most people wonder how a deck of cards can tell you anything about yourself or any other human being. They might call you a cuckoo. What they do not know is that these cards can actually make a difference in changing your perspective on the challenges that you might face in life. This chapter will try to give you reasons why this is true.

History of the Tarot

Tarot reading is an ancient science. It has been said that this practice had originated in Italy during the fifteenth century. It initially was a very popular card game. Many patrons had strived to obtain complete decks in order to win the game. Some of these decks still survive and hold a place of honor in the homes of wealthy patrons. One of the most famous decks is the Visconti – Sforza which was created sometime around the 1450s.

It was in the late eighteenth century when these cards fell into the hands of those who were influential scholars of the occult. They were intrigued by the images on the cards and decided that these images meant more and were more powerful than a simple card game. They then wrote the 'History' of the Tarot. They connected the images on the cards to the mystical systems of Egypt, Hermetic philosophy and Alchemy. The pursuit of seeking knowledge of the Tarot continued into the twentieth century when many secret societies began to include the Tarot in their practices.

The interest in the cards has spread far and wide. Now there are many different perspectives on the Tarot. Multiple decks have been created based on these perspectives. Apart from the original form of the Tarot cards, there are Native American, Dragon and Japanese decks. These decks have become famous over the other decks that have been created in the last few decades.

What can we do with Tarot cards?

The process of reading Tarot cards is very simple. But it is presented in a very dark and cynical fashion. Most films show that Tarot reading is always done in the back of a seedy parlor by n old woman whose face is veiled by the dark shadows. She is seen reading the cards for a young woman or man who is nervous and is worried about what is going to happen to them. The old woman lifts her finger and points at the Death card. The young person gasps and is shocked to learn that their life is in danger. This darkness still clings to the cards. People still worry about entering a place where Tarot reading is held.

Science says that the Tarot cards are symbols of unreason. Science believes that these cards are just a reminder of our unenlightened past. Most religions still shun the usage of these cards. But to learn more about any new idea or concept, we must set aside our apprehensions and start from scratch. What you must remember is that the Tarot cards are just a deck of cards with different pictures on them. The question in your mind could be 'How can we use these cards?' Well, if it is you have come to the right place!

The answer to that question lies with the unconscious. We usually tend to reject the fact that our unconscious has anything to do with how we react to situations. But this is not true. Sigmund Freud has also mentioned in his writings that the unconscious is the abode to all our unacceptable urges, desires and thoughts. We try our best to avoid exploring our unconscious. But it is shown to have a profound effect on us in every way.

There are many ways that have been developed to understand the extent to which the unconscious affects us. Of these, psychotherapy and meditation are the most famous. Over the last few decades it has been found that Tarot reading is another such tool.

A traditional tarot reading has two entities – a reader and a seeker. The reader is someone who has a good knowledge on how to read and interpret Tarot cards, while a seeker is the person with a question. These questions are usually personal questions. Once the seeker has shuffled the cards and cut the deck, the reader places these cards in a pattern. This pattern is called a spread. The reader combines the meaning of the card and also the meaning of the position of the card and tries to answer the seeker's questions.

Meaning of a Tarot Reading

When you are open to receiving or perceiving messages, you will find that there is a message in everything in the universe, right from the trash to the leaves on the trees. Meaning is a quality that is mysterious and comes from the point where the inner and outer realities connect. Each Tarot card conveys different meanings because of its image and the connections between every inch of the image. But it is because of our desire to identify the truths about our lives that gives a meaning to the Tarot cards.

The source of this meaning

It is believed that the meaning to the Tarot cards comes from deep within us. As mentioned above, it is our unconscious that helps us identify the meaning. It acts as a very wise advisor because it understands us extremely well. It is like how Antipater advised Alexander the Great on all political matters. The unconscious knows what we need and leads us in the correct direction. It is known by many names – the soul, the super – conscious, the Inner guide or the higher self. Whatever name it goes by, it is known to have a great connection with the tarot.

Each one of us has this guide. It lays a foundation of meaning for us. Most of us try to cut off this connection that we have with our unconscious. But we cannot, we can only ignore it. You will find that when you reach for the Tarot cards, you are signaling to your unconscious to lead you onto the path of wisdom. This simple act leaves you with the knowledge of the unconscious and the way it provides you with guidance in all matters. In general we forget to dig deeper and only rely on our conscious mind to help guide us.

We will find meaning in the Tarot cards when we give ourselves over to our unconscious. We will be able to perceive the meanings of the cards and also make appropriate choices when we are in a certain situation. But you must remember that you do not need the Tarot cards in order to access your unconscious. For instance take Blu, the Macaw from the Disney film Rio. He assumed that he could never fly. But when he let go and gave himself over to his Inner guide he was able to fly and save the bird he loved. You might not be able to interpret the correct meaning of the cards right away. But keep playing with them, you will find surprise yourself very quickly.

Chapter 4: A Basic History

Tarot is fundamentally a set of playing cards. The most mundane number of cards found in a tarot deck is 78 and the form we currently visually perceive the cards in has been around since the 15th century. The deck of Tarot was first used to play card games around Europe such as tarocchini and Tarot of the French. By the 18th century the decks commenced to appear in utilization by gypsies, fortune tellers and general mystics in the art of divination. Occultists withal commonly use tarot decks as a map of noetic and spiritual paths.

Like any deck of cards, tarot decks have four suits which can vary depending on the region your deck is predicated from. What is the same among all of the decks is what is included with each suit; there are pip cards that emanate from the Ace through the Ten and of course the four Royal cards, King, Queen, Knight and Knave. The deck of tarot withal has a different 21-piece trump suit and one card simply kenned as the dunce. While tarot card games are still widely played throughout European countries, it is the Cumulated States that have a most singular fixate on the cards being utilized for divination and noetic and spiritual maps. Within the purposes of divination the dunce is called the major arcana and the rest of the cards get the title the minor arcana.

Basic Origins

Playing cards as a whole entered the European scene around the 14th century and are thought to have come from Mamluk, Egypt. The suits were akin to the mundane tarot suits of the Swords, the Staves, the Cups and the Coins (withal called the disks and the pentacles). The first indited account of tarot decks in in their painted deck form as we know them today was found betwixt 1430's and 1450's in the city of Milan, Italy. It was at this time that the elaborate illustrations so commonly seen in tarot today began its appearance, taking the tarot deck away from the basic card decks that were in use. These new card sets were titled carte da trion-fi. The oldest surviving cards from a carta da trionfi deck are from 15 elaborate decks that were created for the rules of Milan during the Mid-fifteenth century. None of the decks are intact, but there is enough a sampling to show us the beauty of the artwork that went into these decks.

The Early Decks

While the first documented picture decks came around between 1430 and 1450 it is commonly thought that the decks of cards actually made their first appearance between 1418 and 1425. This thought is because the man who documented the cards Martiano da Tortona mentioned the painter connected to the cards as Michelino da Besozzo who returned to Italy in sometime after 1417 and the commenter Martiano passed away in in 1425 his documentation to be found and published later. In his writing, however he characterizes a deck that has 16 picture cards that have been done in the image of Greek gods with suits that depicted four different kinds of birds.

Decks were often given special motifs and you could find regular packs or those that showed a leaning towards, the philosophical, convivial, poetical, astronomical and of course heraldic ideals. You would also often see, Roman, Greek and Babylonian heroes peppered among the cards. In those early days hand painted cards were the territory of the rich and noble and for the most part (one Dominican preacher aside) there was no taboo or condemnation applied to the cards. One reason for this could be because due to the hand painted nature of tarot cards in those early days there was a limited number of decks created. When the printing machine press came out decks were easier to make and designs became more affordable, the most known of these printing press designs was the Tarot De-Marseille.

How tarot has been used through the years

As we have mentioned the first purport of tarot cards was to play card games. The early set of tarot rules appeared in the writing of Martiano Da-Tortona before 1425 and the next set of rules appeared in 1637. Like any card games the rules can vary slightly from region to region one of the most popular versions of tarot games that is still played today is called Tarocco Bolognese and it is native to Italy. While in France they still play several versions of tarot games and in certain parts of the city you can see public games that tourists can enjoy.

The earliest evidence for tarot being used for divination comes around in a book called The Seer's of Francesco Marcolino-DaForli in 1540. This documentation offers for a simple form of divination of the cards where the cards are used to select a random seer but they themselves have no actual meaning. Compared to the more commonly used use of the pictogram and title, which offers a different concept and archetype depending on the card. It was in writings from after 1734 and 1751 that we found the starts of this more complicated way of divination being used within the cards. They give very basic meanings for each card along with patterns in which the cards should be laid out. It was the famous lover Giacomo Casanova who wrote into his diary dated 1765 that a Russian Mistress of his often used a deck of cards for divination, showing the popular rise in the use of tarot for this purpose.

If you would truly like to dive into the origins and symbols they have been used in the tarot you can try your hand at finding works published by Antoine Court de Gebelin who published several volumes dedicated exactly to this purpose. He never knew the Tarot De-Marseille as the title came later, but with what he had to work with him thought that the Tarot came from Ancient Egyptian works. He felt the decks included pictograms of Isis, Osiris and Seth but he noted Thoth always seemed to be left out of the decks he used the card now accepted as the as the High Priestess as his prime example of Isis.

Chapter 5: Tarot And Its History

This chapter consists of all the information that you should know about card introduction and history of tarot in the world. For spiritual development, perdition, and daily affirmation all related to the tarot cards are worth to read for the tarot players. As an ultimate guide to Tarot, this book will provide you with basic information about how you can perform greatly on tarot with just some amazing tricks and detailed knowledge about cards. We would start learning the Tarot from the arrangement of the cards and the Tarot deck structure. However, before we proceed forward I would like to state the detailed history of Tarot and its introduction in the world. How Tarot was introduced? And how Tarot ancient players were used to play Tarot in their circles is important for your understanding about Tarot.

Introducing the Tarot and History About it

Tarot is a game which is also famous as tarocchi and trionfi. The later was the first name of the Tarot. While on the other hand, the former name (Tarocchi) is the modern name of Tarot. The set of these playing cards was introduced in the middle of the 15th century. Tarot is originated from European countries including Austria, France, and Italy. In the beginning, Tarot cards were limited as the game to play only. However, in the 18th-century Tarot cards were used as a trend for divination via cards reading. Cartomancy leading to custom packs developed for such occult purposes.

Although, some other countries of Europe also claim the historical start of the Tarot. Rather than wasting time to present their evidence and arguments in the support of Tarot origin, I would prefer to conclude that still, we are unclear about the actual history of Tarot cards. Nevertheless, the world agrees that Tarot cards were introduced by European countries in the 14th century. During that time, Tarot cards were commonly played by the people of Egypt and Mamluk with the suit of Polo and Batons sticks. The civilians of these countries were used to practice occult and divinatory Tarot. They named it Wands. The Tarot cards were highly linked with the occult and divinatory tarot in these areas as coins were considered as disks. The entire Tarot cards suits consisted of coins, cups, swords, and baton or polo. Such kind of Tarot suits was also common in traditional Portuguese, Italian, and Spanish communities for divination.

Historical information available on Tarot cards shows that Tarot cards were used for other purposes also apart from playing games as people linked such cards with occult and divination. In the beginning, Tarot cards were 1440 in European countries and 1450 in Ferrara, Bologna, Milan, and Florence. In the advanced Tarot card decks, triumph cards were also added which are now known as carte da trioinfi (in French) and Trumps (in English).

The history of Tarot cards is also projected by the shapes and images painted or printed on these cards. There are some interesting incidents and facts linked with these Tarot cards that are rarely in the knowledge of many card players. In Room card players were used to designing cards with famous iconic leaders and objects. Thus Tarot cards are a way to learn about the history of European countries and the ruling powers of these countries. Around hundreds of years, back painters painted Tarot cards with these famous objects and historical events that are still available in our Museums. You would be interested to know that still, 15 Tarot cards belonging to the 15th century are available in the museum. The suits of these15 cards are known as Visconti Sforza Tarot decks. During the 15th century, Duchy of Milan was the one most powerful ruler in Europe. The suit of ancient 15 Tarot cards was painted for him with colorful attractive objects while considering the interest of a ruler in Tarot cards game. Furthermore, another suit of Tarot cards is available in Museum which belongs to 1420s. Martiano da Tortona's suit of Tarot cards was painted with the images of Roman gods and some kind of common birds of that time.

Pierpont Morgan Bergamo

This deck was painted in 1451 for a colleoni family in Bergamo. The deck was consisting of 70 Tarot cards from which a total of 20 were the trump cards. These cards are available in Academia Carrara and Pierpont Morgan Library. From a total of 74 cards, only 35 are placed in Pierpont Morgan Library, 13 in private collection of Bergamo colleoni family, and 26 in the catalog of Accademia Carrara.

Cary-Yale

The history of Tarot cards is also an attractive topic for the students of history and histologists. A set of 67 Tarot cards dated back to 1466 is also placed in Yale University library since 1967. Tarot cards were included in the Cary Collection of playing cards prior to 1967 as university purchased these cards from them and absorbed in the library of Yale University for the attraction of students belonging to history departments and interested in the study of Tarot cards probability.

As Tarot is originated from Europe, thus it has four major types of suits that represent a specific region. The 4 suits of Tarot cards include Latin suits in Southern Europe, French suits in Northern Europe, and German suits in Central Europe. In each of these suits, there are further 14 cards with different numbering and signs. Ten of these Tarot cards come with numbering on the top or bottom end of the cards. Pip cards numbers start from one and end at ten. Card with number 1 on it is also called Ace. However, after these 10 cards, the rest of the 4 cards are given alphabets and iconic names. The sequence of the remaining 4 face cards is as King, Queen, Knight, and Jack/Knave. Additionally, Tarot cards come with a 21 card trump suit and a single card Fool. Here I would make it clear to you Fool card does not work like its name. Fool card is not always required to avoid playing in a suit. Although, in some suits, it acts as a top trump card and players wish to have it in their cards. Players read this card in two different ways (a card to avoid and a card to trump) which mainly depends upon the type of game being played with these suits.

Reading Tarot cards is predicting the future. When a player reads the card and arranges it accordingly that player actually predicts the future. The stated earlier statements are the common ideas and perceptions about the Tarot in our society. Particularly, people having limited knowledge about Tarot claim such statements. Although, it is a quite false perception and idea about Tarot. In reality, Tarot is just a game of cards with the interpretation of the probability of outcomes. Players of Tarot cards just read the guideline of the cards and make interpretation of probability outcomes on the basis of forces presently at work.

The selection of the first deck is highly important for the players. Many of you interested in the Tarot cards are even not familiar with the right selection of the first Tarot deck. A hundred of possible ways are there but all does not end with a victory or high probability of success. Although, some tricks and tactics related to the Tarot card can work for you. To understand this right selection read this book completely. In each chapter of this book, we have discussed some tactics and strategies which will benefit you while playing with Tarot cards in your friend's circle.

How Reading Tarot Can Benefit You

From the above discussion, we have concluded that Tarot cards are not limited to prediction, in fact, it concerns with probability and interpretation of cards. Reading and interpretation of Tarot cards are not quite simple but believe me, you would find it so interesting and easy with this step to step guide of Tarot cards. Reading Tarot cards can benefit you in many ways. When we talk about benefits an image comes into our mind that relates to the monetary benefit, fame, appreciation, and social status. To some extent, all these relate to the reading of Tarot cards but the most appealing in my views is sensation and feeling of superiority that you enjoy while playing Tarot cards with your social circle. Superiority feelings definitely come in the mind when we do something better than others. Knowledge about Tarot cards and reading these Tarot cards will enable you to always secure a strong and competitive position in the Tarot cards games. You no longer have to put excuses "I don't know how to play it", "I thought it would result in my favour but I was wrong", **and** "It was all the matter of luck. Probably I would perform better next time". Many times you may have made similar arguments and excuses but still, it does not saves you from insult. While I strongly claim that after reading this book and learning Tarot cards reading and interpretation you would be able to show outstanding performance in your circle. You would no longer need to find a new excuse or curse luck on your weaknesses. Read the presented below benefits and advantages linked with the reading of Tarot cards to grab a full understanding of Tarot cards reading and interpretation benefits.

1) Tarot cards are based on archetypes concerning with human conditions thus it provides reflection to our stages of life and states of mind.

2) Tarot cards are being in use for religious instructions from the last 6 hundred years. Thus reading Tarot cards and having

knowledge about it can support you to consult about religious instructions and spiritual insights.

3) Our intuition gets stimulation from the ancient symbols painted on these Tarot cards. By reading these Tarot cards you can strengthen your intuition and practice effective use of intuition in daily matters while deciding about something important related to your life.

4) Through getting understanding about Tarot cards and learning knowledge about Tarot cards reading you can work for social welfare and benefits. Based on this knowledge you can get the capability to empower other people around you to help them find their spiritual paths.

5) Tarot cards reading skills make you capable to see the possibility of an event occurrence. It improves your skills of

realistic prediction and influences your daily life decisions in a positive way.

6) Tarot cards are better-honed intuition and psychic ability. Your psychological condition will be improved and reading cards will provide relief to your mind. Relief and comfort are highly required for our mind and body as our busy scheduled life has a negative consequence for our mental and physical health. Thus, the major benefit of Tarot cards reading is the improvement in psychic ability.

7) Tarot cards reading is a skill that also benefits you while playing other card games. Having skills in Tarot cards you can better understand the rules and tricks of similar games.

8) Tarot cards reading enable you to create a competitive position among your social circle and enjoy the reputation of an intelligent person. Commonly, in our

society, people call intelligence and genius to a person who hardly loses a game and frequently stands first in games. Thus, by reading cards, you would increase your chances of winning as well as to be known as intelligent among your friends. **Is not it interesting?**

9) Tarot cards will also promote your creativity. People having an understanding of card reading and interpretation can creatively present a different perspective on a problem. Conclusively, Tarot cards support self-creativity and innovativeness.

10) It saves you from negative struggles for enjoyment and provides you positive things to do that also increase your skills and make you perfect in problem-solving.

11) Tarot card reading also improves the decision making powers of a person.

The Wrong Myths about Tarot Cards

On the other hand, some people have made a bad image of the Tarot card by spreading some wrong and misguided myths regarding the Tarot cards. To be noted, Tarot reading has been evolving over the history and even though the role of Tarot reading as a physical tool designed for divination is still quite unclear, however, throughout the passage of time, the human beings have applied various different tools, with the main purpose to see what the future has for them. Thus, some people would relate Tarot readings with the ridiculous myths as spread out there days. For this reason, we have to get the exact and detail explanation of those myths, in order to identify that those myths are not actually correct.

It wouldn't be wrong to say that the art of Reading Tarot has brought numerous unnecessary and unwarranted superstitions. If you have been told that drawing out the death card will bring you misfortune, you can rest assured because it is far from the truth.

If you get to ask an experienced Tarot reader about it, you will experience quite a funny scenario. He will really laugh if anyone asks whether Tarot cards are the work of devil. Even though they are frequently asked about it, it never gets old. One of the most common myths is these cards are evil and only a psychic can read them. For instance, you can just ask a couple of people around you and some of them will have the same response.

Not only superstitions are involved with Tarot cards but wrong meanings are associated. For a moment, let's imagine that a death card is revealed when you attempt the Tarot Cards.

What will be your immediate response? You will be undoubtedly horrified. The majority of people will have the same response and that is because they don't know the real meaning of the death card.

Following are some of the common and wrong myths about Tarot Cards:

You shouldn't buy Tarot Cards of your own

Actually, if this superstition was really true, there wouldn't be Tarot readers. It is quite a common myth and you might get to hear about it as well. Some people believe that purchasing Tarot Cards brings you misfortune while some believe that it can make a person deal with the devil itself. It is just a myth and nothing else. And if this was true, what about the shops which are selling these cards?

You can find Tarot cards at a number of shops and they come in different varieties as well.

2. Others shouldn't be allowed to touch your Tarot Cards

It is understandable that you value your cards so much that you don't like when others touch or flick through your cards. However, it is completely different to fear the touch just because you believe it might bring misfortune to you. You have to believe it that it is not true at all. In fact, most of the Tarot Readers don't mind it when people touch their cards.

3. Only psychics can read Tarot Card

Although it is true that Tarot Reading is enriched when the reader is a psychic, anyone can learn this art. Believe me, it doesn't require the reader to make a contract with the devil or anything like that. It is true that one might need training but one can learn it without training by spending a lot of time. I will tell you again that it is possible for anyone to acquire this art. There are no limitations to people who can read the Tarot Cards. Regardless of who you are, you can find a deck of cards.

And as explained above, there are different varieties of Tarot Cards.

4. Tarot Cards are magical

Even though magic is an art in its own. It is quite different from Tarot Cards and you have been misguided if you believe that Tarot Cards are magical. It is true that psychic abilities are in a play when you read Tarot Cards, it doesn't mean that you have to use magic to read them. It is also false that magic is incorporated into the cards.

You have to know that nothing about Tarot Cards is related to magic.

5. They are evil

Another common and wrong myth about Tarot cards is that they are evil. You must recognize that they are not evil and death card doesn't represent bad omen. Regardless of all the rumours of them being evil, Tarot Cards are nothing but cards at the end of the day. They will be assisting a Tarot Card reader in offering guidance to the person. It is actually not possible to utilize them for evil and adverse objectives unless it is the reader who possesses bad intentions.

6. Gypsies invented the Tarot Cards

This is nothing but folklore. There is no evidence worth suggesting that gypsies invented the tarot. Even though its exact origin is not identified, it is also true that gypsies didn't invent the tarot. Hand printed and valuable cards were generally created for aristocrats by people in Europe. Now, they are available to the common public as well.

7. Tarot Cards cannot be wrong

It is true that when a highly intuitive person reads Tarot Cards, it can certainly reveal some possibilities about your future. However, it doesn't mean that you cannot change the future. You are responsible for changing the future. Your choices will play the key role and there is no doubt in it. Tarot Cards can tell you about the possibilities of your future but it doesn't mean that they will always be true.

8. Egypt is the origin of Tarot Cards

One of the most common rumours and myths about Tarot Cards is that they originated in Egypt. Although it was suggested in Court de Gebelin but in 1700s, it was clarified that it was only a mistake and nothing else. There is no relation between Egypt and Tarot Cards. Therefore, if you believe that Egypt is the origin of Tarot Cards, you should stop thinking like that. The origin of Tarot Cards is still not identified.

9. It is not possible to read Tarot Cards through the phone

If you think it is not possible to read Tarot Cards through the phone, you should clear the confusion. In fact, you read the cards over the internet as well. To think that the medium can disrupt the connection between the Tarot Cards and reader is merely a confusion. There is nothing like that and if you have heard otherwise, it is a plain myth. Hence, you should just ignore it.

Overall, these were the most common and wrong myths about Tarot cards.

Trends of Tarot Cards

In recent times, Tarot Cards have become quite trendy and following are some of their most popular trends:

☐Tarot Cards and Happiness

One of the most popular and common trends associated with Tarot Cards is to predict happiness. We all want to know about our future and what will happen to us. And happiness is an emotion that we all love. Just who doesn't want happiness in his life?

Happiness is like many other events which come and go without telling us when they will come back. There are some people who want to be happy but they are unable to feel this emotion because of some specific circumstances. We all face ups and downs in our lives and that is what make them a reality. There is no such thing as a perfect life without sadness as living life means we experience both sadness and happiness. But still, we cherish happiness and don't want to be sad. Imagine that you have been sad for a while now, wouldn't you want to know when you will be happy again?

There is no doubt that the majority of people would want to know when they will get to be happy again. And one can predict this with the use of Tarot Cards. People are increasingly turning towards psychics who can read Tarot Cards to know when they will get to be happy again.

Thus, they use Tarot Cards to predict when they will be more likely to experience happiness.

☐Tarot Cards and Money

Now, most of us thrive and work hard to earn money. There are some people who don't even get the opportunity to utilize their skills and acquire it. You might think that money is an abstract concept and only materialistic people talk about it.

However, that is not quite true.

Just think about it from the perspective of a person who is struggling to earn money. He would be willing to put anything at stake just to acquire it and resolve the issues that he is facing. To him, almost nothing would be more important than acquiring money. Money is similar to happiness in a sense that no one can predict when it might be obtained and when it might be lost. Hence, the knowledge of one's money status can be quite helpful in planning for the future.

For instance, if you were to what your financial status would be in the future, how would you feel about it? You would certainly feel enlightened and would have a ton of options to take. If your financial status is going to degrade, you can take some effective steps to avoid the situation or plan for it in a better manner. And if you get to know that you will be acquiring money in the future, it will help you ease your worries and be a little stress-free in the present time.

It is, however, important to know that even though it is a trend and you might follow it as well, you shouldn't take some serious steps like not working on your future once you have a glimpse that you will get money in the coming time. It can adversely influence your future.

Tarot Cards and the Future

For a long time now, we have been watching programs and reading stories about people who go into the future. In the future, they find what they did wrong and whether they are living successfully or not. If they are not happy or successful, they go back to the past and try to change what they are doing in the present. It helps them in changing the future. What if you could do the same?

Wouldn't it be awesome if you could just know about your future? It would certainly be great. And one of the popular trends about Tarot Cards is that people use them to know about their future.

It is true that Tarot Cards are capable of letting you know about a little bit of your future. Even though they are not completely right, they are not completely wrong as well. This can help people in knowing a little about what they will be doing or what will be happening to them in the future. For instance, you might get to know that you will take a successful step in the future towards your career. If you are fortunate, you might also get to know what you can do to make the prediction come true.

In this manner, you can know about your future. Thus, this curiosity causes people to use Tarot cards to know about their future.

Tarot Cards and Flaws

People spend their lives without knowing what issues exist in them. They don't even know in which direction they should be putting their attention to improve themselves.

If we get to know about our flaws and just what we are missing, we can get an opportunity to work on ourselves and how we behave, act, and work. We will be enlightened about all of these aspects and we will also get to know just what we are lacking. For instance, one might be effective in working and might be honest but he might not be focusing on communicating with others. He might believe that he is doing the right thing by focusing on his work but he can improve himself by concentrating on his communication and interaction with others.

If he works on this particular aspect, he will be capable of not only improving but also growing himself. What if you could also get to know about what you are lacking? It would help you identify the issues and flaws that you couldn't spot before. Moreover, it would aid you in focusing on those aspects and nurturing yourself.

There would be countless options for you to take. You can do it with the help of Tarot Cards. This has become one of the most popular trends in the present. And you might find people who are interested in knowing about their flaws.

Connection to Astrology and Kabbalah

Speaking of Tarot, in which there are total 78 cards constitute the structure, it would be quite essential to consider the arrangement of these cards, or else, inside the **Hermetic Tree of Life**, and to view them as symbolic representation of the tree in the context that considered as a form of book, thus, Tarot has also famous as the Book of Life. As lots of people around this world have sided off the learning of Kabbalah with the reason of one perception which mentioned that this study is quite complicated to be learned and understood. Yet, if you have been interested in the matters of the soul, aim to get the proper understanding around Tarot, astrology, and around our universe itself, then the Kabbalah combines all of these together. The reason is due to Kabbalah contains astrology, dream, numerology, healing, quantum physics, holy geometry, medication, and definitely, the **Tree of Life**.

The Kabbalah has been present for thousands of years, and its highest fundamental texts titled the **"Sefer Yetzirah"** or more famous as the **"Book of Formation"** discusses the entire impacts that the planets could influence on us, the human beings. All the primary arcana included in Tarot resemble an astrological symbol or else planet, and the primary arcana was conventionally assumed to have been passed over to the human beings by the Archangels, in accordance to the Kabbalistic education. The **Tree of Life** which is basically a figure which has been presented as the universe's DNA placed its special position at the core of Kabbalah.

The **Tree of Life** consists of simple notes whereas every one of them connected to a planet or rulership, same as a chart of astrological. The tree is constructed of **10 spheres**, along with Sephirot, the emerging one, alleged together by the universal rules within three stakes. Even though 22 paths are attaching the spheres, on the other hand, there are some hidden paths as well. This tree has been reflected as a map of this universe and covers every single thing that has ever presented into reality, or else will be formatted with the rise from **Kether** (the crown).

Despite the fact that Kabbalah integrates Tarot and astrology, it is considered against the principles in Kabbalah teaching if we would use these only to make some predictions. Instead, both Tarot and astrology are actually the tools made for human beings to understand properly the spiritual perspective which is natural in each circumstance. The Kabbalah teaches the human beings that our souls will keep on return again and again as we all pass through the entire tree, and to some extent, we have turned out to become one with heavenly. The Kabbalah as well has been emphasizing free will as to how we could understand our souls better by using all the Tarot symbols together with astrology, whereas our energy then has the potential to be concentrated positively in certain ways that would able to benefit ourselves and other people as well. Furthermore, Kabbalah has insisted that we need to learn who we really are and which things that we could achieve before we could start to figure out about the spiritual matters.

Figure 1 - The Tree of life

The Tree of Life, no matter how detailed and complex it is, but still, it is incompetent in transmitting all of the information. However, this Tree of Life could be quite pleasant to view if you know exactly what you are viewing in a specific **'multidimensional'** method right after placing over the various diverse astrological, tarot, mythological, numerological, and symbolic layers. In the context of Tarot, this Tree of Life has been considered as an effective map of the human soul, an image which symbolizes the powers of **Nature**, **Consciousness**, and of course, the **Universe**.

The most essential thing that we should understand around Kabbalah is quite obvious and simple: the real definition of Kabbalah is **'receiving.'** In Kabbalah, we are dealing with the creation detail in the contexts of a sincere God. The Kabbalistic system has a foundation which mentioned that our loving God has created the universe that we are living in, as well as created us as creatures who have the capability to accept, with the tender responsiveness and sensible gratitude. All of us have options to make, even though we are born perfect, but we could eventually collapse into evil ways. According to the Kabbalistic system, the Tarot cards are actually a vehicle of certainty, in which all of these 78 illustrated cards are assumed to acquire their own roots in the most primitive spiritual tradition of Jewish. The images configuration along with the symbols embedded within the Tarot cards replicate the ancient cryptic knowledge of Kabbalah. For this reason, the Jewish believe that by discovering the historic roots along with the Kabbalistic components of the Tarot, that we would able to originate the most real and completest definition from these ancient tools. Even in these modern days, the practices of Tarot cards reading is quite famous as the most popular technique of fortune-telling. The reason might due to the fact that Kabbalah has brought up the concept that it precedes any type of religion in this universe, and thus, it is an amazing revelation from God to human beings.

In the contexts of astrology, it is obvious that Tarot and astrology are deeply connected. The difference between them is that, in astrology, readings and the zodiac symbols put more focus on the planets along with their positioning. On the other hand, the Tarot reading puts focus more on the mythical supremacy of the astronomic world. Combining both Tarot and astrology will assist the Tarot experts along with the reads to extend their practices. In fact, there is an assumption mentioned that every single of the Tarot card within the Tarot deck has a relation with astrology. One of the extreme connections between the Tarot and astrology was arranged with the rise of the **Order of the Golden Dawn**, which is a cryptic order that was intensely linked with astrology and spirituality.

Chapter 6: What Is Tarot?

The Tarot (also known as Tarock, Tarokk, Tarot, and similar names) is a family of trick-taking card games. The game has expanded to 78 cards, which contain legal documents for each of the four semi-regular dress, to win a permanent 21 cards, and a kind of "wild card" with the name "mad" or "I'm sorry." Even Though it is regarded primarily by many as a means of predicting the future or divination, the Tarot deck was created in Northern Italy during the 15th century as play cards. The idea of winning a suit that survives in such popular card games as spades and Hearts comes from the Tarot game.

The myth of the Egyptian origin of tarot cards, although once common, has long been revealed by later scholars, before the eighteenth. For centuries, there is no trace of tarot cards used for occultism or prophecy. Popular tarot readings at Renaissance fairs are a creative license taken with a historical fact and should not be considered authentic. Contrary to popular belief, classic playing cards were not derived from Tarot card games, and the Fool is not related to The Joker of classic playing cards. The Joker was created in the United States during the 19th century originally for the card game Euchre.

There are two types of Tarot deck.

The appropriate Italian Tarot

The traditional game of Italian, suitable for coins, cups, swords, and batons, is currently favored by those who use Tarot cards, divination. However, in some countries such as Italy and Switzerland, these decks are still used for the game. Those who practice tarot prophecy often call coins "pentagons" and "wands." With a few exceptions, trump the Italian Tarot adapted the scene varies little from one platform to another and are often regarded by Tarot readers as containing a symbolic meaning. The depiction of Papessa (II) and the pope (in) on related Italian Tarot Cards has been controversial in some regions. In Switzerland, these images were replaced by images of Juno (II) and Jupiter (V.). In Bologna, the papal figurines with Empress (III) and Emperor (IV) were replaced by four figures of moresche, which are not numbered and serve as triumphs of the same status in the Bologna Tarot variety. The system of Italian or Spanish costumes is not limited to tarot cards. This suit system is a common regional model of classic playing cards in southern Europe and Latin America.

French tarot

Tip card with a French or international outfit, tiles, heart, spades, Clover is now used in countries such as France and Austria for the game. In France and southern Germany, Roman numerals have been abandoned in favor of Arabic numerals, while in some countries, such as Austria, Roman numerals are still used. Trump Images appropriate to the French Tarot often depict scenes of people at work and play, and real and mythological animals and landscapes, the regional space. In some regions such as Austria and southern Germany, the game is reduced to 54 cards with the removal of the lower pip card. Unlike the relevant Italian decks, there is a wide variety of images on French tarot cards. On the decks of the French Tarot, a mad man is often depicted as a musician, harlequin, or other types of artist. French Tarot Cards are rarely used for divination.

Common rules of the game

At each turn, players must follow, if possible. If the seeds are not possible, it will be necessary to reproduce the resource. If the players are empty in the suit played and are also empty in the cards, then any card can be played. The winner of one round leads another.

There is a noticeable variation in how a fool or an excuse is used. In countries like France and Italy, The Fool is a "wild card" that can be played in any order, to avoid having to follow suit, while in some countries like Austria and South Germany, the Fool is simply the biggest asset.

Many modern tarot games include offers to determine who will become the recipient and play alone against other players. In some tarot cards with four or more players, the recipient of the card called the king or the high-ranking card chooses a partner, whose identity remains secret until the called card is played.

The values of Cards where "n" is often equal to 1, 2, 3 or 4 depending on the type of game played, are presented as follows:

Trump XXI (21), Trump I (1), the excuse or the fool, and the four Kings are worth 4 + 1 / n each

The four queens are worth 3 + 1 / n each

The four Knights or Knights are worth 2 + 1 / n each

The four sockets are worth 1 + 1 / n each

All other cards have a value of 1 / n each

The usual goal of Tarot card games is to score more card points, as well as any other bonus point, which may also be available depending on the regional variant you are playing.

Tarot reading and divination

Although they were originally designed for card games, Tarot Cards are generally regarded by many as a splitting tool, especially in regions where Tarot card games remain largely unknown. There are many published bridges that are dedicated today for the purpose of divination. The most famous bridge designed for divination or "getting information" is the Tarot Rider Waite Smith.

Using fortune-telling cards, they are arranged in a pattern. These patterns, usually in the form of a cross, are known as "throws" or "spreads." "Queerer," which is the one who aspires to read the tarot cards, mixes the package and asks the question in the cards. The question could be "yes" or "no" of a more general type or nature. The reader organizes the cards into the proliferation of choice and allegedly tries to answer the question using the cards as a guide. The divinatory interpretation of a Tarot card often depends on the vertical or inverted direction of the card or its juxtaposition with other cards. Sometimes only 22 cards from the Tarot deck are used. These cards, called "Major Arcane" by Tarot readers, include 21 triumphs and one Fool. The remaining 56 cards are called "minor arcane."

Not all Tarot readers call themselves "fortune tellers" when they claim not to use cards for predictive purposes. In recent years, "psychological" rather than paranormal interpretations have been guided by a context in which a lot of tarot data is visible. These tarot data are called "introspective" in nature and do not make supernatural or prophetic statements. Tarot reading has recently become popular in some circles as a reflection tool in an attempt to increase your creativity. It should be noted, however, that there is no empirical evidence of psychic phenomena or therapeutic benefits of Tarot data.

Chapter 7: Suit Of Cups

There are fourteen cards in the suit of cups. There's the Ace, Two through Ten, Page, Knight, Queen, and King. When you've pulled a card from the suit of Cups, the immediate topic being brought to light is one of the emotions involving relationships both romantically and spiritually. However, it doesn't always have to do with relationships we share with others, but the relationship we share with ourselves. The element commonly associated with the suit of cups is water, and the zodiac signs are Cancer, Scorpio, and Pisces.

 Here are the following meanings for the Suit of Cups cards in a tarot deck.

Ace of Cups

When the Ace of Cups is drawn in the upright position, it symbolizes compassion, love, overwhelming emotions, and creativity. If it's reversed, it signifies repressed or blocked emotions.

Two of Cups

The Two of Cups upright symbolizes partnership, attraction, and unified love. When it's drawn reversed, it meaning there's an imbalance in a relationship that may lead to a break-up, and there's a lack of harmony between two people.

Three of Cups

The three of cups upright signifies friendships, celebrations, community, and creativity. Reversed it stands for three's a crowd, stifled creativity, and an affair.

Four of Cups

The four of cups upright represents feelings of contemplation, apathy, meditation, and reevaluation. Reversed, this card represents someone who is bored, has been aloof and feels they've missed an opportunity.

Five of Cups

The five of cups upright symbolizes someone who's suffered a loss, feels regret, disappointment, bereavement, and despair. Reversed, this card means someone has moved on and expressed acceptance as well as forgiveness.

Six of Cups

Six of cups upright signifies someone who is experiencing childhood memories, nostalgia, reunion, and innocence. Reversed, this card symbolizes someone who is unrealistic, naïve and stuck in the past.

Seven of Cups

The seven of cups upright represents those who are living in a fantasy or illusion, and those are practicing wishful thinking. It also stands for someone who must make a choice and has an overactive imagination. Reversed, this card symbolizes temptation, diversionary tactics, and illusion.

Eight of Cups

The eight of cups upright represents disappointment, escapism, and abandonment. Reversed, this card symbolizes hopelessness, someone who is walking away or aimlessly drifting.

Nine of Cups

The nine of cups upright symbolizes comfort, fulfillment, wishes, and happiness. Reversed, it represents materialism, greed, and dissatisfaction in life.

Ten of Cups

Ten of cups upright represents marriage, harmony, and happiness. It also represents an alignment between two people. Reversed, the card symbolizes a broken home or marriage and a misalignment of values.

Page of Cups

The page of cups upright symbolizes creative beginnings, synchronicity, and someone who is a messenger of good news. Reversed, the card represents a creative block and someone who is suffering from emotional immaturity.

Knight of Cups

The knight of cups upright signifies a knight in shining armor coming to the rescue, charm, romance, and a vivid imagination. Reversed, the card signifies someone who is moody, unrealistic, and jealous.

Queen of Cups

The queen of cups upright symbolizes someone who is experiencing calm in their life, emotional security, and compassion. They're also very intuitive. Reversed, the card represents someone who is codependent and insecure.

King of Cups

The king of cups upright represents a person who is balanced and in control both emotionally and physically. They're also very generous. Reversed, the card symbolizes someone who is moody, volatile, and emotionally manipulative.

Chapter 8: History Of Tarot Cards

The first tarot cards were created as a game called triumph with 22 special picture cards that were like trump cards similar to bridge in Europe. According to How Stuff Works, in 1781 occultists in France and England looked at the trump cards and saw additional meanings in them and began using them as divination cards they called tarot starting 1953 because the Italians called them tarocchi and that was the French version. There are many kinds of tarot cards and decks drawn by many people, you can even draw your own deck if you so choose. There are fairy decks, dragon decks, Celtic decks, shapeshifter decks, Egyptian decks, and nature decks, but the most common deck is the Rider-Waite deck in the US. The many different kinds of decks allows for people to choose what is right for them, what style they like the best and goes with their personality, and which deck resonates with them on a personal level.

There are no same number of cards among decks, nor do the drawings look similar at all, although the suits and types of cards are the same and the meanings are very similar.

The Rider-Waite deck is 78 cards made by a member of the Hermetic Order of the Golden Dawn. It has a major and minor arcana. The arcana are separate decks of cards. The minor arcana are similar to a regular deck of playing cards in that they have four suits numbered ace (1) through 10 and they each have court cards, although there are four court cards instead of three. In a regular deck the cards number ace through 10 and jack, queen, king in the suits of clubs, diamonds, hearts, and spades.

The minor arcana tarot deck numbers 1 through 10 with a page, knight, queen, and king, and the suits are wands, swords, cups, and pentacles (or circles). The minor arcana cards deal with mundane, minor, general life issues. The major arcana cards have no suit. They are numbered 0 - 21, so have 22 cards. And the deal with the major life events people go through. For instance if you got a major arcana card about something and then followed by a minor arcana card about the same or similar thing, it takes on smaller importance than if you just go the major arcana card. And each deck can take on hundreds of meanings depending on how the cards are laid down together and what spread is used.Also each person has their own interpretations of the cards and what they mean to them.The meanings of the cards can even change with the times, depending on the culture of the person doing the reading, and the needs of the person doing the reading. The older decks seem to have little relevance to our modern world, but the newer decks seem to be harder to interpret. The original decks depicted pictures that the people of the time understood because they were things that could actually happen to them.

Tarot is a form of divination, but as with any divination tool, it is only a possibility of what could be. You make choices and can influence your own destiny. Being shown a possibility gives you the chance to choose differently, to make your own fate.

Chapter 9: Understanding Tarot

This section of the book will walk you through various ins and outs of the tarot cards. If you are curious to learn about the details of the deck in detail then this portion is perfect for you. Here, you will learn about different cards, the spread and readings.

So, without further delay – let's get started.

The Cards

There are 78 cards in the tarot deck and their illustrations are interpreted in multiple ways. There are two divisions of the tarot cards. These are called:

Major Arcana

Minor Arcana

There are 22 trump cards in major arcana while the minor arcana is divided into four suits. These are known as:

Wands

Pentacles

Cups

Swords

Each suit has got cards with numbers 2 to 10. Moreover the suit also consists of four court cards (the Knight, the Page, King and Queen) and an ace. This means that each suit consists of 14 cards in total. If you look at it from a different perspective you will realize that, these suits correspond to clubs, hearts, spades and diamonds in playing cards.

The Concept of Card Meaning and Intuition

There are a lot in tarot instructors who encourage students to develop a proper psychic intuition. This implies that intuition is preferred over conventional card meanings. However, if you merge the card meanings with intuition then you can have the best results from the reading. Thus, it is recommended that you rely on both the meaning and intuition while reading the cards.

Intuition guides the reader to the image present on the card. Moreover, it can also suffice to establish connection with the environment. These two factors can contribute towards reading the tarot cards in an efficient manner.

For example,

Empress Card – pregnancy

Tower Card – Loss of Job, divorce, any other disaster or tragedy

Five of the Pentacles – Financial Hardship or Poverty

Six of Pentacles – Generosity or Charity

These meanings can be derived straight from the intuition but if you know the meanings then you will be able to make a better judgment via the cards. The reader has a whole bunch of options when he knows the meanings of the cards and does not rely on the intuition alone. Thus, it is recommended that you make use of meaning and the intuition while reading tarot cards.

Negative Cards Meanings

It is a common among the beginners that they get scared or a bit hesitant when they come in contact with the negative cards. In general, people don't like to see the Death, Tower, Devil, the Ace of Swords or the Hanged Man. This is because of the fact that these things can mean something negative.

In amidst of this discussion, it should be noted that these cards appear often as these incidents are part of our normal life. However, these cards can often prove to be positive as well. For example, the death card can also indicate transformation into a better person with an improved career and impressive life.

One of the main problems for the reader is to convey the meaning of negative cards to the seeker. In this regard, different readers go for different strategies. Some of the readers try to refrain from delivering the bad news while some tell the duration of ordeal and use passive means of delivering the news.

It can be really difficult to avoid the negative cards particularly when someone wants to be considered an accurate reader. A tarot reader can be considered as a priest or spiritual advisor. People always have the option of praying however they often exert themselves to seek advice from people like priests or tarot readers. This happens especially when an individual is in an intense state or some tragic scenario.

If you are giving a good reading to someone then it means that you are being a really good therapist to him. In other words, you can either save him by reading the tarots or demotivate him. You should be exerting yourself to explore a person and be the listening ear throughout the process. You can rely on various things to motivate a person and perform his therapy in a much better way. In this regard, offer a prayer, rely on intuition or take guidance from spiritual guides. But, sometimes the problems indicated by the cards are way more than the reader can or should handle. In such a case, it is advised that you refer the seeker to some professional expert.

Tarot Layouts or Spreads

The way in which the cards are placed on the table is known as layout or spread. It should be noted that in each spread – every card has a particular meaning. The most common one is the Celtic Cross.

As far as the recommendations for various types of layouts or spreads are concerned, it should be noted that different people propose different ideas. Some people are of the opinion that the readings should be performed on a wooden table rather than some other material. This is due to the fact that wood reflects vibrational energy. Moreover, a quiet room is more preferable as compared to a noisy one. On top of that, it is suggested that the reader meditates before each reading.

You should take care of the fact that the cards are to be placed with citrine or other crystals. This ensures that the energy stays clean. Another fact about tarot cards is that they can be read almost anywhere. A lot of tarot readers have confessed this. However, the results are highly dependent on the fact that how much a reader is concentrating and what is the amount of intuition received.

Shuffling

There are many methods of shuffling. Different tarot readers propose different methods based on their experience and mostly intuition. One of the most important methods is to concentrate on the question of the seeker while shuffling. Based on the intuition and experience, you can follow the given method.

Concentrate on the seeker's question

Shuffle the deck in such a way that you follow your intuition

As a matter of fact, you should keep in mind that following your intuition is very important during the whole process.

Moreover, here are some more suggestions.

Make choice that who will cut the deck

If the seeker wants to cut the deck then explain to him that he should cut it into three pieces. Tell them to do it in such a way that they feel right about it. This would make them do it properly rather than getting confused by the term "intuition".

If you decide to cut the deck yourself then you should go along with the same process. Cut the deck where it feels right. In other words, follow your intuition.

Once the deck has been cut into three piles, it is to be noted that either you or the seeker has to choose a particular pile. Again, let your intuition guide you while making this choice. If you decide to choose the pile then ensure that you choose the one which you feel to be correct. In other case, if the seeker wishes to choose the pile himself then guide him to choose the one which feels right to him. In the scenario that you feel that he has not made the right choice then you can always pick up the right pile and set it aside. Later, if you realize that the reading is not correct then maybe you could refer to that pile and tell the seeker that this might be the right one for you.

Once done, start to lay out the cards from the top of the chosen pile. Some readers prefer to place the cards upside down and read them as the process goes on. You can also do that but feel free to put them with their face up (if your intuition says so).

After laying out, you are all set and ready to start reading.

The Celtic cross Layout

It is one of the most common claims that this layout is the most powerful amongst all. This is mainly because of the reason that it is used vey frequently and is very active is releasing some form of collective energy around it.

The pattern to lay the tarot cards is shown below.

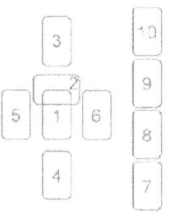

Some of the readers do not deviate from using this form of layout as they strongly believe that it is most effective in producing results. While other readers are of the opinion that each layout has its own purpose and meaning.

The European Layout

Since, you are starting out as a beginner – it is suggested that you choose this layout to practice reading the tarot cards. Based on the simplicity, it can prove to be a really good starting point. Here is the description of the spread.

First group of three cards (1-3) – reflect the person's past

Second group of cards (4-6) – reflect an individual's present

Third group of cards (7-9) – reflect the seeker's future

In other words, the complete timeline stretches from the far past to the distant future. Take card number 1 as the oldest experience in someone's life while card number 9 would be something that will happen in the distant future.

Other Layouts

It should be noted that there are numerous other layouts for the tarot cards. Once, you are good with these spreads you can try the other ones as well. Keep in mind that it all depends on intuition and you should go for whatever feels right.

Chapter 10: Types Of Readings

Before you start reading tarot cards, you need to able to put them into a position called a spread. Just like tarot decks, there are also tons of tarot spreads available. But we'll settle for the much more basic and simple ones for now. Why do you need to learn how to spread the tarot cards? Well, each spread possess a different kind of information. While other spreads gives the reader a year view and even some astrological perspectives. All the spreads offer information, but some highlight the information that might really matter to you like emotional issues.

Five Card Spread

The Five Card Spread helps the people know what course of action to take next. As it says on the name, you take five cards and place one in the middle. Next, you place one card on each side of the middle card, it kind of looks like a cross now.

Card 1 (in the middle): the general theme of your reading.

Card 2 (left side): represent some past issues that still affect the present.

Card 3: (right side): shows the future.

Card 4: (bottom card): the main reason behind the question, it can even help give more information about number 2.

Card 5: (top card): all the potential within the situation.

Subconscious impulses are shown in card number 4 or even something that's stopping you from achieving what you want. While card number 5 show some possible result if they do take the course of action. It's better if you focus on the aspect of your possible decision while choosing your cards.

The Eclipse Spread

Another spread that helps answer your questions is the Eclipse Spread, which is made up of seven cards. The first card should be placed first on your left side, continue placing the next card next to the first one. The rightmost side should have the seventh card, it should also look like a wide V where the first and last card are aligned. Also, the middle or fourth card should be the lowest one.

Card 1: Past events that still influenced the current situation.

Card 2: All the influences that surround you as of the moment.

Card 3: Future influences that may weigh in the situation.

Card 4: What you need to do right now.

Card 5: All the outside forced or influences that have effect.

Card 6: All your hopes and fears.

Card 7: This represents the possible result of the situation.

The most crucial card in this situation may be the fourth one, the answer to your problem or question.

The Celtic Cross

This one might be a little difficult and confusing since it has ten cards, but it is actually one of the most common and used card spread. The Celtic Cross is the best spread if you want some of your specific questions answered.

First step is to create a Five Card Spread on your left side. Next is to take the second card and place it on the middle card of the Five Card Spread. Take note that when you place it above the middle card, it should be in a horizontal position. Lastly, take your remaining cards and form a vertical line on the right side of the Five Card Spread. The tenth card should be the one on top, the seventh in the bottom.

Card 1 (middle of the Five Card Spread): Represents the present

Card 2 (card placed on top of the middle card): This represents the immediate challenge that you face. A challenge that you need to overcome. But if you have a good card here instead, think hard because it still represents a challenge.

Card 3 (right card in the Five Card Spread): The root of the problem found in the distant past.

Card 4 (bottom of the Five Card Spread): A much more recent past, this also includes some events. This may not be the min root of the problem, but it's fairly connected.

Card 5 (above the Five Card Spread): The best possible outcome, though it still can't compare to card number 10. However, if this card is a negative one, you should cut your losses immediately.

Card 6 (left card in the Five Card Spread): The immediate future which indicates the next few days or weeks.

Card 7 (bottom of the horizontal card): Possible inner feelings that greatly affect and influence the situation.

Card 8 (above card 7): All the possible external influences. This may be people or events that can't be controlled.

Card 9 (above card 8): The hopes and fears regarding the situation or problem. This card can be confusing most of the time. If it gets too confusing, draw another card and evaluate both of them.

Card 10: The outcome, usually a self-explanatory card. Though if it proves to be also confusing, you should draw three more cards for clarification.

The Relationship Spread

It's pretty obvious what this spread is for. Though the 10 cards it requires can be a bit confusing to set up. The first in a step is to place five cards straight in a horizontal position. The first card should be on the left, the fifth card on the right. Next step is to place card number six above card number three.

Take card number seven and place it below card number three and four. Card number eight should be under two and three, beside seven. The last two cards should be placed above card number six. Nine on the left and ten on the right.

Card 1: Represents the distant past.

Card 2: The recent past.

Card 3: Shows the present.

Card 4: Future situations that has an influence.

Card 5: External factors that influence the situation.

Card 6: The attitude of the one possessing the problem.

Card 7: All the helpful energies present.

Card 8: Obstacles that need to be solved.

Card 9: All the hopes and fears associated with the situation.

Card 10: The final outcome.

Chapter 11: Cups And Wands

Ace of Cups- There is a potential for love if you follow your intuition but don't forget about your spirituality.

Two of Cups- There is a great chance for a new partnership, it could be romantic or business, you shouldn't need to feel reserved about this partnership because both parties are working towards the same goal.

Three of Cups- Take joy in the success that is coming your way.

Four of Cups- You have been too careless disappointment is coming. You should focus on moderation in your life.

Five of Cups- Your life is out of balance and if you continue on this path you will suffer from great sadness.

Six of Cups- Now is time to reflect upon the past before moving into the future.

Seven of Cups- You will be faced with temptation but you need to make a choice. Make sure what you choose is not based upon a delusion.

Eight of Cups- It is time for self-discovery you may find it is time to start making some sacrifices.

Nine of Cups- Satisfaction is coming your way. You will have a time of abundance in your life. Enjoy it.

Ten of Cups- Everything you do in life right now will be blessed and will bring you great joy.

Page of Cups- It is time for new beginnings in your life. Use your imagination and create all that you want.

Knight of Cups- There are messages that you need to open yourself up to, this is a time for calmness in your life.

Queen of Cups- You have great insight that needs to be shared with those around you. Watch out for things being done in secrecy because they will be brought out into the open.

King of Cups- You may have sympathy for those around you but you need to make sure you are not putting them before yourself. Everything needs to be done in moderation right now.

Ace of Wands- Your health may be unpredictable right now but do not spend your energy focusing on it. Instead spend this time being creative.

Two of Wands- Your will power is at its highest right now. You can do anything you want in your life so make those changes right now.

Three of Wands- Now is the time for you to benefit from all of the strength you have shown in the past respect yourself and you will be successful.

Four of Wands- It is time for you to take a step back and spend some time getting your life in order. If it is rest you need take it but don't take too much time resting, now is the time for achievement.

Five of Wands- It is time to decide what your priorities really are not doing so could cause conflict in your life.

Six of Wands- It is time for recognition in your life but don't let your confidence turn to arrogance.

Seven of Wands- You need to prepare yourself for what is coming in the future but don't allow your bravery to determine which path you will take.

Eight of Wands- Transformation is needed in your life and you have the energy right now to do what it takes!

Nine of Wands- You have the potential for progress in your life if you don't lose your stamina.

Ten of Wands- You may feel burdened by your new found responsibilities but with determination you will be able to release these negative feelings.

Page of Wands- Right now you are fearless, you feel as if there is nothing you cannot accomplish but take heed you are not invincible and should proceed with caution.

Knight of Wands- You need emotional support right now and you need to make sure you are building up a support system of those who truly care about you. Don't allow yourself to be deceived.

Queen of Wands- You are full of ambition right now but you need to make sure that you are consistent or all will fail.

King of Wands- Vision is what guides you and you are a great leader, accept the role with pride. Make sure compassion is not forgotten.

Chapter 12: The Connection Between Tarot And Astrology Card Combination

There is no denying that soothsaying and tarot are profoundly connected. The two methods of reasoning counsel the astral world for direction. While in crystal gazing, zodiac signs and readings center more around planets and their situating, tarot centers around the legendary intensity of the astral world. Joining soothsaying and tarot helps tarot professionals and perusers grow their training, while for customers, the two methods of reasoning assistance advance their life. Some accept that each card in the tarot deck identifies with crystal gazing. Discover the associations among soothsaying and tarot here.

The Genuine Association

As a general rule, crystal gazing assumes a significant job in the elucidation of the cards and the implications in tarot. The spread in tarot regularly resembles a group of stars. Perhaps the greatest connection among crystal gazing and tarot was set with the rise of the Request for the Brilliant First light, a recondite request that was profoundly associated with soothsaying and otherworldliness. A few decks have risen because of crafted by this request, including the Thoth tarot, the Brilliant First light tarot, the BOTA tarot, and the Rider-Waite-Smith tarot.

How Are Crystal gazing and Tarot Extraordinary?

One thing that is unique with regards to soothsaying and tarot is their notoriety. Soothsaying is measurable and is firmly identified with arithmetic. In the times of the Roman Realm, celestial prophets were really called mathematicians. All things considered, crystal gazing makes individuals have a sense of security, as it tends to be determined. Tarot, then again, has its very own perusing and significance, and it is frequently extraordinary relying upon the peruser. The very embodiment of tarot is free elucidation, and the announcements are drawn from agreeing circumstances. A few people believe that an intelligently determined celestial perusing is substantially more exact and has a more strong establishment than a tarot one.

Crystal gazing and Tarot: The Zodiac

As per devotees to both tarot and soothsaying, zodiac signs are each connected to a tarot card from the Major Arcana. The connections among crystal gazing and tarot cards are as per the following:

Aries is connected with The Emperor, a card speaking to unwaveringness.

The card of the Taurus is The Hierophant, speaking to information and individuals looking for higher facts.

Gemini is connected with The Sweethearts, speaking to the equivalent double nature of picking between the high and the low street.

Malignancy, or The Chariot, speaks to the affection for being free and beating life's contentions.

Leo's card is Quality, speaking to mental, physical, enthusiastic, and profound power and fearlessness.

Virgo is connected to The Loner, speaking to a need to back off and concentrate deliberately throughout everyday life.

Libra's card is Equity, a perspective where individuals set up their sentiments and feelings aside to settle on a reasonable choice and result.

Scorpio is connected to Death, and this sign invites change and change.

Sagittarius and its partner Balance are talented go betweens and frequently discover their way through challenges.

Capricorn is connected to The Villain, encouraging individuals to consider antagonism and swap it for certainty.

The card of Aquarius is The Star, concentrating on confidence and helping individuals around them to accept that the sky is the limit.

Pieces is connected to The Moon, an animal of regularly evolving states of mind.

Chapter 13: The Key To The Major Arcana

THE MAJOR ARCANA

The basic contrast which exists between the minor and major arcana is that in the last the photos, numbers are united, while in the previous they are particular. There are 22 significant arcana, yet one of them bears a 0, so that, in actuality, there are just 21 extraordinary or major arcana. A large portion of the creators who have considered the Tarot have dedicated upset their consideration regarding these 22 cards, without seeing the others, which, be that as it may contain the genuine key to the System.

Be that as it may, we will leave these deviations and begin the use of the law Yod-he-vau-he to this bit of the Tarot. A little reflection will recommend to us that there ought to be some arrangement in the major arcana just as in the minor arcana. In any case, how are we to characterize the points of confinement of the individual arrangement? Each card of the minor arcana bears an image that effectively associates it with the entire plan (Scepter, Cup, Sword, or Pentacles); it is distinctive in the other option case. Each card bears an alternate image.

In this manner it isn't imagery that can manage us here, at upset occasions for the occasion. Other than the image, each card communicates a thought. This thought is of itself a superior guide, for it is simpler to arrange than the image, however, such guide doesn't yet upset the security that we could want, for it might be perused diversely by different people. Once more, the thought continues from the activity of the image upon the other term communicated by the card—the number.

The number is surely the most dependable component, the most effortless to follow in its advancements, it is, hence, the number that will direct us; and through it, we will find the two different terms. Give us now a chance to review our clarification of the numbers, and we will effortlessly characterize the arrangement of the major arcana. Be that as it may, from the beginning we should make one incredible reservation.

The arrangement which we are about to identify is the most common, however, they are not just ones. All things considered, we will currently think about the four first major arcana. The numbers 1, 2, 3, 4 on the double show the order to be received and the idea of the terms.

1 -relates to Yod, and is dynamic.

2 -to He, aloof.

3 -to Vau, fix.

4 -to the second He, and shows change.

This fourth Arcanum relates to the Knave and to the 10 of the minor arcana and becomes Yod in the next or following arrangement. On the off chance that we wish to make a figure of the main ternary 1, 2, 3, we ought to do it thusly 1 two different terms are at different points. This ternary can likewise be spoken to in with Yod-he-vau-he, (3)1 triangle, the affinities

1 yod 2 he, second he, 4 VAU and Second Ternary. We have expressed that the 4 becomes the Yod or dynamic term in the accompanying grouping.

The 4, speaking to the Yod, in this way demonstrations with seeing to 5 and 6 as the 1 acted with respect to 2 and 3, and we get another ternary. The 7 demonstrations here as the 4 acted already, and the same rule applies to all the arrangements in the arcana.

FIRST SEPTENARY

The use of one law to altogether different terms has driven us up until this point; we should not relinquish this System, however, continue on and state. In the event that in one ternary exist a functioning term = yod, a latent term = lie, and a fix term = vau, coming about because of the two first, for what reason ought not a similar outcome be found in a few sets of three taken together? The main ternary is dynamic and relates to yod; the subsequent ternary is uninvolved and relates to lying; the response of one ternary upon another brings forth a third ternary or vau.

On the off chance that we characterize the similarity between this first septenary furthermore, the Yod-he-vau-he, Ave will discover. A conclusion might be made in going from which a lot of data will be inferred, on the off chance that it be painstakingly contemplated. The 4 is just the 1, considered contrarily, the 5 is just the 2 considered adversely, while the 6 is the negative of 3. It is consistently the same number under various perspectives. We have consequently characterized a first septenary, shaped of two contradicting sets of three.

We have seen that this septenary additionally replicates Yod-he-vau-he.

SECOND SEPTENARY

The law that applies to the first sets of three is additionally valid for the others, and following a similar strategy we get a subsequent septenary, in this way shaped Positive Ternary Negative Ternary. The two sets of three, positive and negative, will adjust each other to bring forth a subsequent septenary and to its term of progress, 13. Subsequently In any case, if the two sets of three separately go about as positive also, negative, for what reason ought not the two septenaries do the equivalent? The principal septenary, taken in general, will accordingly be sure, moderately to the subsequent septenary, which will be negative.

The principal septenary relates to YOD, the second to lie. Third Septenaky. The third septenary is hence shaped. In the event that the principal septenary is certain and the subsequent negative, the third will be fixed and will relate with vau. We ought to have subsequently, certainly

First, A POSITIVE SEPTENARY = Yud.

2nd, A NEGATIVE SEPTENARY = He.

3rd, A NEUTER SEPTENARY = Vau.

However, every septenary contains one term which has a place to the previous septenary, and one which has a place with the accompanying septenary. Subsequently, the 7 is the seventh term of the principal septenary, what's more, the first term of the second. 13 is the last term of the subsequent septenary and the first of the third, and so forth. The outcome is that three terms stay to be classed. These are 19 _ 20 — 21. These three terms structure the last ternary, the ternary of change between the major arcana and the minor arcana, a ternary which compares to the subsequent he, also, which might be along these.

The last numbered card, which should accurately to bear the number 22 (or its Hebrew journalist), shuts the Tarot by a glorious figure, which speaks to its constitution to the individuals who can get it. We will come back to it by and by. In this manner, in the major arcana, the incredible law is in this manner certainly spoken to. The primary septenary compares to the Divine World to God; The second to Man; The third to Nature; At long last, the last ternary demonstrates the entry from the Creative and opportune world to the world of predetermination. This ternary sets up the association between the major and minor arcana.

Chapter 14: Tarot, Numerology, And Qabalah

Numerology

It is this vibration that gives each number different characteristics and affects our lives in different ways.

The core of Numerology believes that nothing in the universe happens by coincidence or accident, but rather, it is the vibrational energy of numbers that cause things to happen a certain way.

The historical influences of Numerology go as far back as the Greeks with the creation of Pythagoras Numerology by the one and only Pythagoras himself. In addition to the creation of the Pythagorean theorem, Pythagoras was fascinated with the idea of the vibrational frequency of numbers. Pythagoras subscribed to the idea that numbers connect all things – a revelation that began with the discovery that adding up odd numbers starting with one will always result in a square number.

After this revelation, Pythagoras continued his research by studying the mathematical ideals of Arabic, Druid, Phoenician, Egyptian, and Essene sciences.

It is his subject of Numerology that we will be focusing on today, as it is the most widely used and considered.

Pythagoras was a brilliant man who formulated ideas that are still widely used and acknowledged today, but he was also incredibly secretive. He taught a school in Crotona, Italy, called the "semi-circle" and was treated more like a secret society.

With Pythagoras forbidding his students from writing his teachings, it makes it difficult today to research him as very few of his original writings still exist. However, this wasn't the only secret society devoted to Numerology. In fact, we now know today that Numerology had a hand in many secret societies. From Masons to Rosicrucians, the study and belief of numbers having a deeper connection to the world are highly valued. While Pythagoras paved the way to our modern-day Numerology, he was not the sole creator. Not by several thousands of years.

It is widely debated on who or which community created Numerology first, but what is very interesting is that they all seem to have come to the numerological conclusion on their own. Many ancient societies have their own versions of Numerology, and all of them developed it without truly communicating their ideas to one another.

The earliest records we know of today trace back to very early Egypt and

Babylon, but we also have evidence that very early in Chinese, Roman, and Japanese history, Numerology was studied and used. In the modern age of Numerology, there is a different person who is credited with bringing Numerology out of its cave and into the public eye. Her name is Dr. Julia Stenton, and she is credited with the resurfacing of Numerology in modern-day studies.

In fact, she coined the term "Numerology" for a study of names connected with numbers that had previously been unlabeled. Stenton came to this term by combining the Greek word for 'Numerus' or 'Number' and 'Logia' to mean thought or expression.

Numerology has fascinating connections to Tarot and the Zodiac as each of these methods of divination have numbers assigned to them in different ways. The

Zodiac, for instance, has a number associated with each of the star signs depending upon its order in the Zodiac lineage.

Each Tarot card also has a number associated with it that has a deeper meaning than just its location within the deck. Because of the numbering on each of the Tarot cards, they each have their own distinct meaning within Numerology that gives even more depth to the already very complicated understanding of each card. The number one, for instance, is often associated with new beginnings or the start of something – and there are five cards in a deck of Tarot that are numbered one.

These are the Magician card, the Swords, the Ace of Wands, and the Pentacles. And while all of these cards have very different distinct meanings, they all connect in some way to beginnings and fresh starts. People often think of Tarot and Numerology as a cycle, with even numbers typically being sturdy and dependable while odd numbers usually represent some sort of state change or transition.

Because of this cyclicity, many numbers can often have multiple meanings, as the end of one thing can mean the beginning of another.

Numerology's connection to the Zodiac is exciting and not as evident as its connection with Tarot. While the connection with Tarot is right in front of your face on the cards, Numerology's connection to Astrology lies in the action behind understanding Astrology itself.

In order to understand or create someone's birth chart, you must consult their birthdate and time – all numerical values that have great importance in that person's life. In addition, you must then consult the constellations, which you need to know different degrees and longitudinal and latitudinal information about in order to understand fully.

At the base of all of this information is numbers that play a huge part in understanding the personality and inner self of a person. Astrology, while appearing at first glance to be mental and not based in the physical realm, is in fact based very strongly in mathematics and science.

Within Numerology itself, each number from zero to nine is ruled by a planet much like the Zodiac in Astrology. It is often when doing a reading of a person that the individual will take both their Zodiac and numerical value into play as each depends and informs one another about the person.

In the next chapter, you will learn how to calculate your numerical values and what each of them mean for you as well as some real-life examples of how your numerology can affect you with certain situations and times.

How Numerology is connected to Tarot

Tarot is a great realm to finally acknowledge that truth. Furthermore, that 3rd trick suggested that by memorizing the numerological associations, remembering major themes in your deck becomes easy and so much more accessible. The details of those associations will be revealed below.

Remember that every card is associated with a number, and most decks will print the number directly on the card for your ease. The Major Arcana number from 1-22 (or 0), and the Minor Arcana go from Aces to Kings, which technically number from 0 to 14.

The Meaning of 0 (Zero)

Zero is said to represent all that exists as potential in the universe. 0 is the connection we share with everything else through the simple fact that we exist. We are here now, and that means we can be anything. 0 reveals that potential. 0 also demonstrates the concepts of connectedness, understanding, and wholeness.

The Meaning of 1

Number 1 is said to represent new beginnings, taking initiatives, and finding a simple sense of completion. It is a number fulfilled in itself, and it has its own internal balance that doesn't depend on anything else. 1 demonstrates the promise of something good coming, and it also relates to one's powers of manifestation.

The Meaning of 2

Number 2 is said to represent one's relationships with others. It signifies connectivity, intimacy, and romance as well as platonic relationships of all sorts. 2 is about interplay, interactivity, and the choice you have within all those different options. 2 demonstrates all that experience with others has to teach you.

The Meaning of 3

Number 3 is said to represent what happens as a product of union. 2 is about that union in many senses, but 3 reveals the creative product, result, or outcome. 3 is the essence of creativity and expression. Furthermore, it demonstrates the path of growth. 3 illustrates the importance and value of synthesis.

The Meaning of 4

Number 4 is said to represent stability, home life, and structure. 4 is all about what happens under 4 walls, or what becomes complete with a 4th line: the square. The square additionally symbolizes numerological perfection in some ways. 4 is a number that exists within nature too as a backbone and stabilizer, so it demonstrates this material world we inhabit.

The Meaning of 5

Number 5 is said to represent both health and crisis in health. It is the same number as there are points on a star, which relates to the pentagram (associated with selflessness and goodness) and the pentacle (its inverse, associated with self-focus and variability). 5 is a divine number that reveals a transformation will come;

however, it also demonstrates the extremes of that transformation potential.

The Meaning of 6

Number 6 is said to represent natural harmony or balance, and it is another number that suggests a union is in order. In this case, 6 represents the divine marriage between divine masculine and divine feminine, which can take place within each individual as well as between individuals in the world. It's a number that demonstrates connection and the integrated knowledge that will emerge from it.

The Meaning of 7

Number 7 is said to represent magic itself. 7 is the number of mysteries, the occult, the divine, and what remains hidden (although often in plain sight). This number correlates with expanded education on many levels, too, whether that occurs through self-guided study, spiritual practice, metaphorically going back to basics, or literally going back to school. In sum, 7 demonstrates what can happen when you experiment, take risks, research, and develop your own inner magic.

The Meaning of 8

Number 8 is said to represent abundance itself. 8 is also a manifestation number that's intimately connected with the divine. In many pagan calendars, 8 holy holidays were celebrated, and 8 still represents the number of seasonal holidays we hold dear. 8 demonstrates the importance of worship and celebration, as well as all that comes from that: prosperity and the essence of abundance.

The Meaning of 9

Number 9 is said to represent completion that aims toward leadership. You are following a cycle that's about to be completed, and that will mean new options for you. 9 signifies this energy. Furthermore, 9 demonstrates what happens when you're entirely selfless and allow yourself to be directed by divinity. 9 is about the healing that can be enacted for self and others when you're openly loving.

The Meaning of 10

The Number 10 combines the energies of 1 and 0; it is said to represent new beginnings like the number 1, but it's more importantly about how endings are often new beginnings in disguise, using that vital energy of 0, too. 10 is a number of culmination and things ending. It is also a number that demonstrates freshness and transformation.

The Meaning of 11

The Number 11 combines the energies of 1 and 1; it is said to represent spiritual awakening. In the tarot, 11 associates with Pages from the Minor Arcana and with the Justice card from the Major Arcana, but the number itself represents intuition, inspiration, and connection with one's higher self. 11 demonstrates the importance of listening both to one's inner voice and to the voices of the world in order to establish ethics, morality, direction, and a sense of righteousness.

The Meaning of 12

The Number 12 combines the energies of 1 and 2; it is said to represent new beginnings based on liberation, independence, and self-reliance. In the tarot, 12 associates with Knights from the Minor Arcana and with the Hanged Man card from the Major Arcana, but the number itself represents what happens when you realize your life purpose and/or soul mission: everything fake fades away, and you become the most authentic version of yourself possible. 12 demonstrates that capability.

The Meaning of 13

The Number 13 combines the energies of 1 and 3; it is said to represent one's powers of manifestation. In the tarot, 13 associates with Queens from the Minor Arcana and with the Death card from the Major Arcana, but the number itself represents that what seems harsh may be exactly what you asked for. 13 shows you how your circumstances are more of your making than you may have realized before, yet it also demonstrates potential to break new ground with this realization.

The Meaning of 14

The Number 14 combines the energies of 1 and 4; it is said to represent a warning regarding money matters and that some test may be coming soon. In the tarot, 14 associates with Kings from the Minor Arcana and with Temperance from the Major Arcana, but the number itself represents sacrifices you may have to make if you desire to achieve your goals. It demonstrates beneficial challenges ahead that will result in lasting successes.

The Meaning of 15

The Number 15 combines the energies of 1 and 5; it is said to represent your increasing awareness that positive change is coming. You're about to realize what's been holding you back all along, and that may be painful, but you'll emerge stronger than ever. 15 reminds you to keep your eyes on the prize so that you aren't held back by the struggles that lay ahead. It demonstrates resilience, strength, needed transformation, and introspection.

The Meaning of 16

The Number 16 combines the energies of 1 and 6; it is said to represent material success to come. 16 is all about your ability to turn obstacles into positive outcomes, and the number suggests that you may find the next example of this ability sooner than you thought. 16 encourages you to have faith and stand strong, for it demonstrates how your willpower will win out after all.

The Meaning of 17

The Number 17 combines the energies of 1 and 7; it is said to represent an aspect of leveling up in your life. For the most part, 17 relates to leveled-up manifestation experience. Your intuition will be your greatest guide through this adaptation, but remember that significant changes are imminent! 17 demonstrates how you'll have to step up to the plate for this leveling up to occur.

The Meaning of 18

The Number 18 combines the energies of 1 and 8; it is said to represent increased discernment, wisdom, and confidence. The outcome of such positivity will be increased capacity for abundance, which works well after 17 gave you all the manifestation experience you could need. 18 will encourage you to use all that abundance for the benefit of mankind, too. 18 is selfless, if not somewhat idealistic, and that is a beautiful combination.

The Meaning of 19

The Number 19 combines the energies of 1 and 9; it is said to represent something similar to what number 10 does--showing us that endings often provide the best and freshest new beginnings. 19 is the number that reveals your divine purpose and connects you with that experience. It's about the inherent stability that can be provided by self-help, and it demonstrates the changes you can incorporate into your life when you are able to face your darkest sides.

The Meaning of 20

The Number 20 combines the energies of 2 and 0; it is said to represent that harmony is coming your way as long as you live with compassion, love, and connection to your intuition. 20 also encourages action with others that validates these gifts of compassion, love, and intuition. Through appropriate action, harmony can be established, and 20 demonstrates that beautiful and liberating potential.

The Meaning of 21

The Number 21 combines the energies of 2 and 1; it is said to represent pure energy in expression, whether verbally, physically, or metaphysically. 21 is a manifestation number as well as a transformative one, and it encourages taking new directions with your new modes of expression. 21 accompanies charisma and genuine communication with others, demonstrating a more evolved version of the self.

The Meaning of 22

The Number 22 combines the energies of 2 and 2; it is said to represent accomplishment and acquired power. 22 is also a number representative of successful partnerships, but this could have pertinence for one's vocational endeavors more so than romantic ones. 22 demonstrates how confidence and hard work pay off and how blessings abound when a harmonious life is achieved.

Conclusion

Thank you once again for purchasing this book.

This is the book you must refer to if you are a beginner. It provides you with all the necessary information you must know when learning about the Tarot – from the history to the cards in the deck. It also helps you understand the meaning of the cards in the deck. It is best to use the spreads that are mentioned in the book! Helps you learn quickly.

You must remember that you are a beginner and that you might make mistakes in the beginning. But that is okay! As a child, while learning to ride a bicycle, you kept falling. But you always got back to your feet and began to ride again. Remember that when learning to read and interpret the Tarot Cards. If you are unsure of yourself, start giving yourself a reading before you give another person. Initially it is best to use the Three Card spread since that is the easiest and you would not make a mistake.

The different cards have all been described in detail and should help you in the process. Since there are 78 of them, you might take a little time to understand it. However, with time and through practice, you will know their meanings by heart and will be able to speak about them without having to refer to this book. The basic idea is for you to have a spontaneous telling session that will help your customers get a good reading and be happy.

But remember: don't give away a very grave reading, which might start them to worry. Try and keep it honest and simple and always end the session on a positive note. They have come to you because they trust you and you have to fulfill your promise of giving them a true and reliable reading.

Enjoy your journey and use it wisely.

www.ingramcontent.com/pod-product-compliance
Lightning Source LLC
Chambersburg PA
CBHW071448070526
44578CB00001B/255